Englisch-Stars

4

Erarbeitet von

Barbara Gleich
Irene Reindl
Katrin Schmidt
Britta Schöpe

Illustriert von

Martina Mair und
Wilfried Poll

Inhalt

📕 Read the comic.

Back to school

✏ 1. Fill in the correct sign (< , >). ☑

twenty 〇 twelve

fifteen 〇 thirteen

fourteen 〇 nineteen

eleven 〇 sixteen

eighteen 〇 twenty

seventeen 〇 fifteen

Setze das richtige Zeichen ein:
❯ (größer als) oder
❮ (kleiner als)

✏ 2. Find the words. Write. ☑

thirteen

-teen

Welche Zahlwörter haben die Endung -teen?

4

3. How much is it? Fill in. ✓

In Großbritannien bezahlt man mit pounds = £

The helicopter is _thirty_ pounds.

The teddy bear is _____ pounds.

The computer game is _____ pounds.

The inline skates are _____ pounds.

The dress is _____ pounds.

The boots are _____ pounds.

The T-shirt is _____ pounds.

The shoes are _____ pounds.

The jeans are _____ pounds.

| twenty | thirty | forty | fifty | sixty |
| seventy | eighty | ninety | one hundred | |

I love shopping.

5

1. Find the words and circle them. Fill in. ✓

Suche die Wörter senkrecht und waagrecht. Kreise ein. Trage dann unten die durcheinandergeratenen Wörter richtig ein.

k	o	b	a	t	h	r	o	o	m
z	g	c	d	o	o	r	z	k	l
g	a	u	h	i	y	t	i	w	r
f	r	e	a	l	b	g	y	w	b
n	d	h	r	e	v	w	e	i	e
a	e	k	i	t	c	h	e	n	d
z	n	d	e	s	h	f	x	d	r
h	k	g	a	r	a	g	e	o	o
j	s	t	a	i	r	s	b	w	o
l	i	v	i	n	g	r	o	o	m

living room	**toilet**
bedroom	**stairs**
kitchen	**bathroom**
garden	**window**
garage	**door**

 Lucy is cooking in the **ikcehtn** _____ .

 Mum is watching TV in the **vngiil mroo** _____ .

 The car is in the **ggraae** _____ .

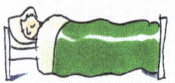 Dad is sleeping in the **dbrmooe** _____ .

 Kevin is playing in the **nraged** _____ .

 Emma is taking a bath in the **ohatobmr** _____ .

 Sally is reading on the **otielt** _____ .

2. What is it? Complete and draw lines. ✓

Was hat sich hinter den Bildausschnitten versteckt? Vervollständige erst die Wörter und verbinde dann mit dem richtigen Bild.

ch _ _ r

_ ab _ _ _

_ e _

l _ m _

c _ _ bo _ r _

s _ _ _ _ _ _ s

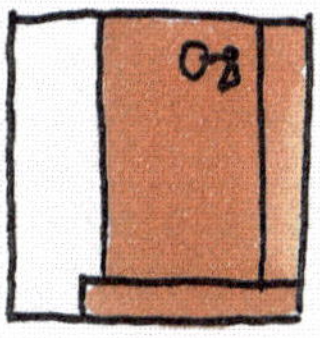

_ es _

s _ f _

lamp
table
bed
sofa
cupboard
shelves
desk
chair

3. Find the furniture and colour the fields brown. What can you see? ✓

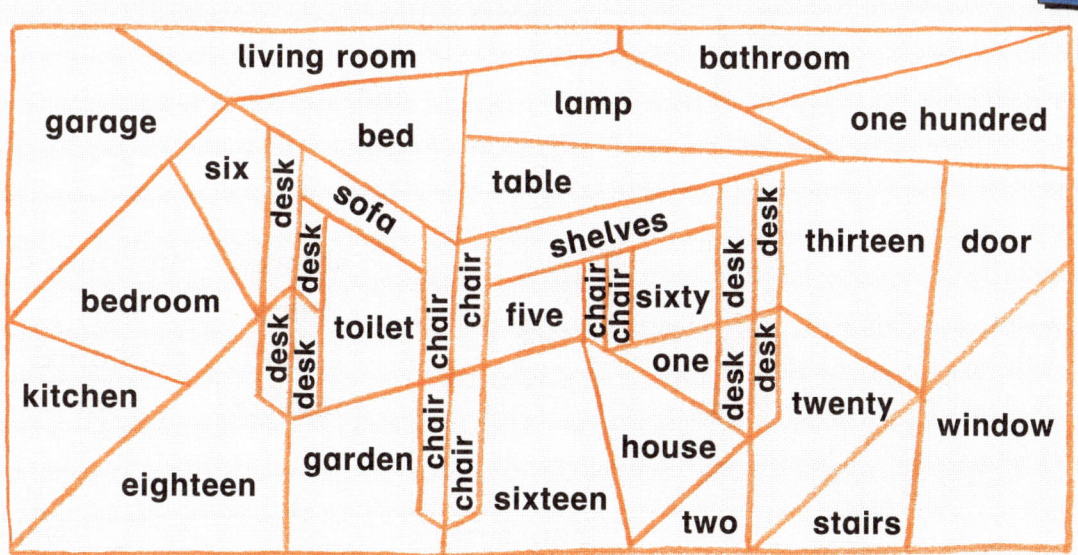

I can see a _____ .

7

 4. Describe the rooms. Fill in.

Was gibt es alles in den verschiedenen Räumen zu sehen? Schreibe auf. Passe bei cupboard und cupboard<u>s</u> auf.

In the _____ there's a _____ and

two _____ .

bedroom
kitchen
living room

In the _____ there's a _____ ,

a _____ , a _____ and three _____ .

shelves   cupboards
lamp   bed
chairs   cupboard
table (2x)   sofa

In the _____ there's a _____ with

four _____ and a _____ .

8

5. Crazy rooms. Read and number. ✓

Welche Beschreibung passt zu welchem Zimmer?

○ My room is purple. I've got a table with three chairs and a pink bed. I've also got a pink toilet and a small garden.

○ My room has got a small bed, a small desk with a chair and two big shelves.

○ I live in a very dark room. In my room there's a red sofa and a black cupboard. I don't like lamps.

9

6. Read the comic.

Is there a room for me?

1. Find the words. Draw lines and write.

mustard	lettuce	ham	cheese	bread	ketchup
	tomato		cucumber		

2. Read and draw lines.

I like a sandwich with tomatoes, cheese and cucumbers.

I like a sandwich with mustard, ham, lettuce and ketchup.

I like a sandwich with ham, cheese and lettuce.

3. What is it? Read and write.

It's brown and soft.   It's _____ .

It's green and long.   It's a _____ .

It's yellow and a mouse likes it.   It's _____ .

It's yellow, but it's not cheese.   It's _____ .

It's green and has got leaves.   It's _____ .

It's pink and part of an animal.   It's _____ .

It's red and looks like a small ball.   It's a _____ .

It's red, but it's not a tomato.   It's _____ .

bread	tomato	cheese	ham	cucumber	ketchup
		mustard	lettuce		

4. Write and draw lines.

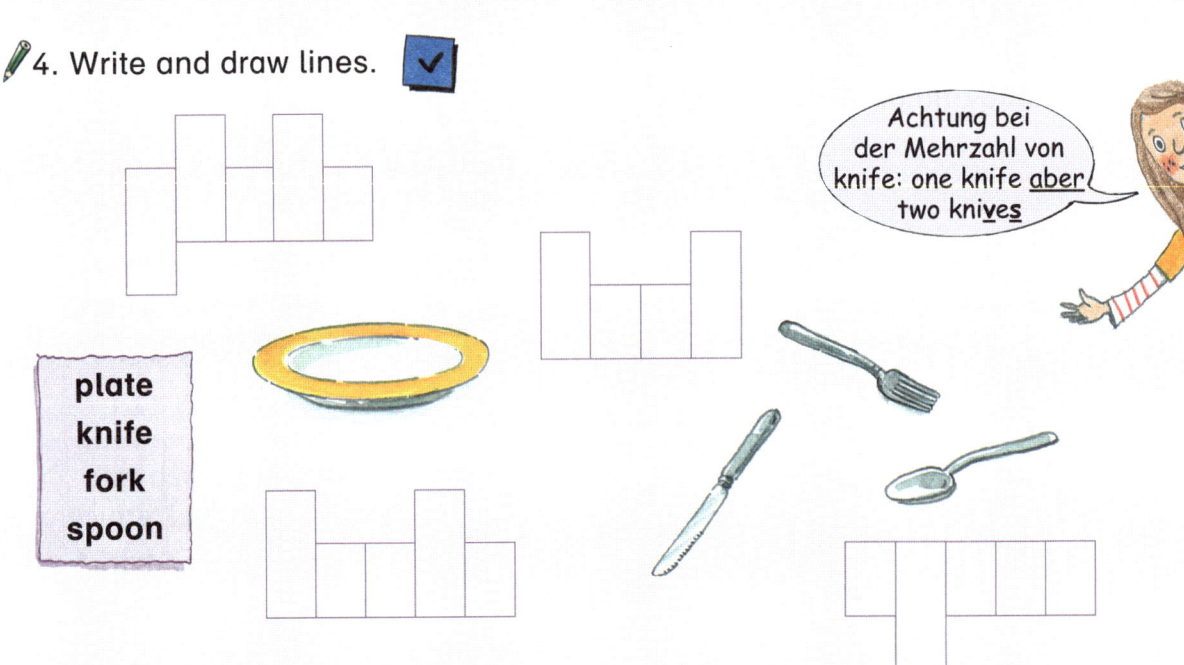

plate
knife
fork
spoon

Achtung bei der Mehrzahl von knife: one knife aber two knives

123 🖊 5. What's on the menu? Number and write. ✓

1. **carrot soup**   £3.00
2. **pizza**   £5.00
3. **spaghetti**   £5.50
4. **fish and chips**   £5.00
5. **sausage with mashed potatoes**   £7.50
6. **chicken salad**   £4.50

🖊 6. Do you know what the children want? ✓
Write.

> Die bestellen ja alles völlig verdreht! Schreibe es richtig auf.

 I'd like spaghetti soup and a carrot.

_____ .

 I'd like a fish salad and chicken and chips.

_____ .

 I'd like a mashed carrot and a sausage soup with potatoes.

_____

_____ .

7. Complete the dialogue. Write. ✓

What would you like to _____ ?

We'd like a _____ _____ and a _____ , please.

Would you like something to _____ , too?

We'd like a _____ and a _____ , please.

Here you are.

_____ .

That's twenty pounds.

_____ .

pizza   drink   eat   **Here you are**   **Thank you**
coke   lemonade   **sausage with mashed potatoes**

14

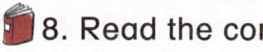 8. Read the comic.

Sally likes lollipops

Zeichne die Uhrzeiger richtig ein und spure dann die Sätze nach.

 1. Draw the clock's hands and write.

It's
two o'clock.

It's
six o'clock.

It's
eleven o'clock.

 2. What time is it? Write.

It's three o'clock.

nine	eight
five	three
twelve	

 _____ .

 _____ .

 _____ .

 _____ .

3. Write and draw lines. ✓

Lucy's day

get up   play with my friends
do my homework   have breakfast
go to bed and sleep   go to school

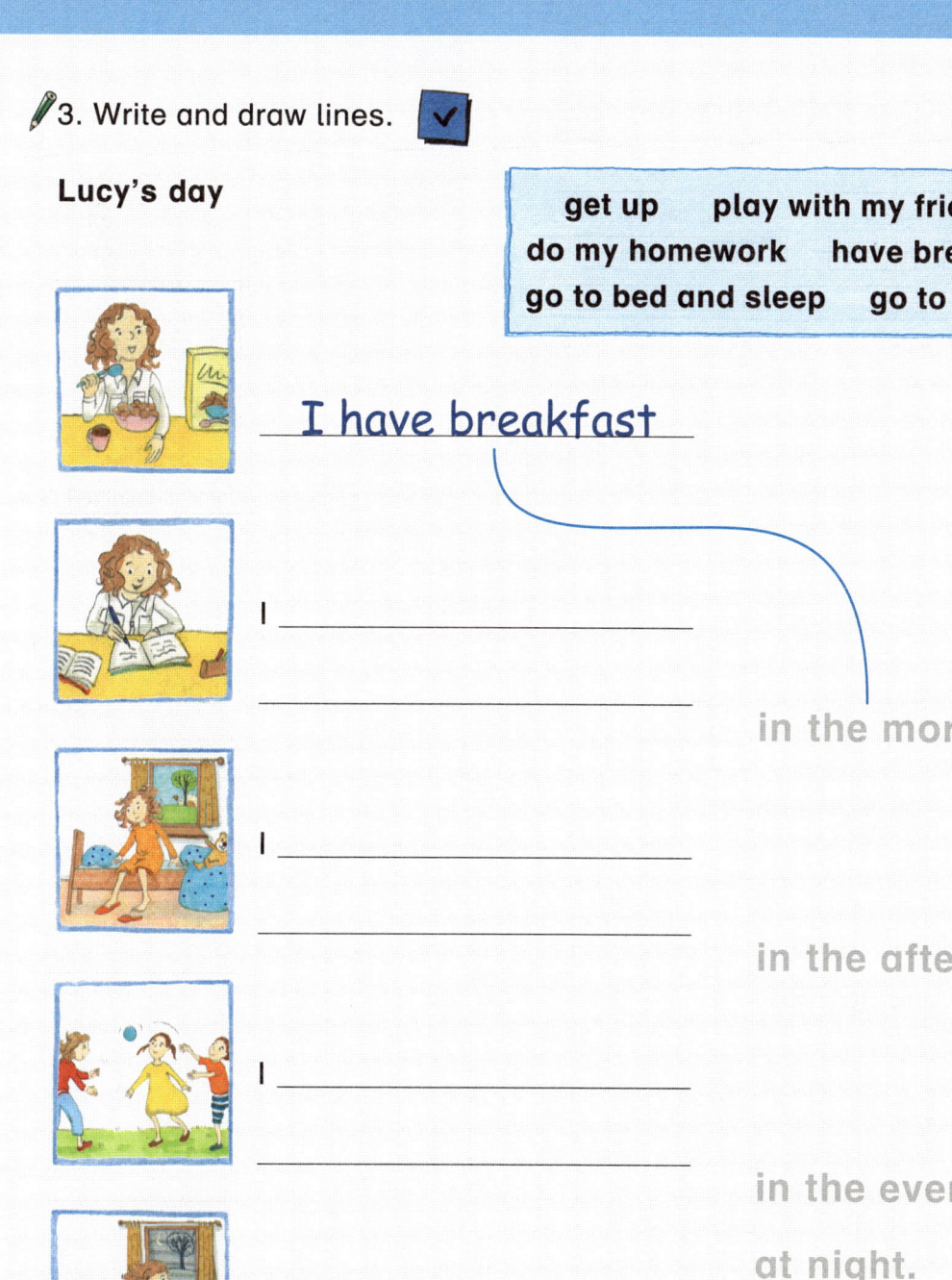

I have breakfast

I _____
_____

in the morning.

I _____
_____

in the afternoon.

I _____
_____

in the evening /
at night.

I _____
_____

I _____
_____

 4. An interview. Read and fill in. ✓

Hello, Ben.   Hello,

                                 _____ (your name).

When do you get up?   I get up at

                                 _____ o'clock.

When do you start school?   I start _____

                                 _____.

When do you do your   I do my _____
homework?
                                 _____.

When do you play with your   I play with my _____
friends?
                                 _____.

When do you go to bed and   I go _____
sleep?
                                 _____.

Thank you for the interview.   You're welcome.
Goodbye.   Bye.

5. Read the comic.

Time for breakfast?

1. Trace the lines and write.

_____ likes **riding a mountain bike**.

_____ likes **reading books**.

_____ likes **swimming**.

_____ likes **riding a horse**.

_____ likes **playing football**.

_____ likes **snowboarding**.

_____ likes **playing the piano**.

_____ likes **ice skating**.

_____ likes **playing the guitar**.

2 Guess the hobby. Read and write. ✔️

> My favourite hobby is playing an instrument. My instrument is very big. I can play a lot of songs on it.

Sam

> In summer it's the perfect hobby. I jump into the water and I'm happy.

Betty

> For my hobby I sit on an animal. The animal likes to eat grass, apples and carrots. It's a big animal.

David

Ron

> I can do my favourite hobby wherever I want. I only need a book.

Kathy

Linda

> I do my hobby in winter. I go to the mountains. I love snow.

> For my hobby I need a ball. I hit the ball with my feet.

Linda's hobby is _____ .

Ron's _____ .

Betty's _____ .

Sam's _____ .

Kathy's _____

_____ .

David's _____

_____ .

| snowboarding | reading books | riding a horse |
| swimming | playing the piano | playing football |

21

3. Look at the pictures and write. ✓

Jane   Harry   Bill

Can Jane play tennis?   _Yes, she can._

Can Harry play football?   _No, he can't._

Can Jane ice skate?   _____

Can Bill ride a horse?   _____

Can Harry play tennis?   _____

Can Jane play the guitar?   _____

Can Bill play basketball?   _____

Can Harry swim?   _____

Can Bill ride a skateboard?   _____

Denke daran: Verwende bei Jungen **he**, bei Mädchen **she**.

And what can you do?

I can _____

_____

 **4.** Read and fill in.

 Hello. What's your name?

 Hi. My _____ is Tom.

_____ your name?

 _____ is Helen.

What's your favourite hobby?

 My favourite _____ is _____

_____ .

What's your _____ ?

 I like _____ , too.

Let's play together!

 Good idea! Let's go!

And I like playing football, too.

23

1. At the shopping centre. Write.

In the supermarket I can buy _____ .

In the music shop I _____ .

_____ .

_____ .

_____ .

_____ .

_____ .

_____ .

| orange juice   CDs   books   shoes   lollipops |
| pullovers   inline skates   teddy bears |

2. In the clothes shop. Write.

Are the clothes just right?

No, the jacket is too big.

Yes, the dress is just right.

_____.

_____.

_____.

too big	too small	just right	pullover	dress
	shoes	skirt	jacket	

Wem gehört welcher Einkaufskorb? Ergänze die fehlenden Dinge.

3 In the supermarket. Whose shopping basket is it?
Add the missing things to the list. ✓

Sarah
coffee, eggs, _____

_____

_____

George
bananas, milk, _____

_____

_____

Andy
pineapple, ham, _____

_____

_____

Olivia
bread, coke, _____

_____

_____

butter	honey	lemonade	bacon	cherries	tea	spinach

jam   milk   oranges   water   chocolate bars   eggs   rolls

cheese   apple juice   cornflakes   biscuits

 **4. In the sports shop. Read and number.**

 It's £30. ◯

 Here you are. Goodbye.

 Thank you. Bye.

 Here are the skateboards. Do you like the colour? ◯

 No, sorry. I don't like red.

 Hello. Can I help you? ◯

 Hello. I'd like a new skateboard.

 Do you like the green skateboard? ◯

 It's perfect. Green is my favourite colour!

 5. Read the comic.

Sally goes shopping

1. Find the correct word. Write.

$\overline{3}$ $\overline{1}$ $\overline{15}$

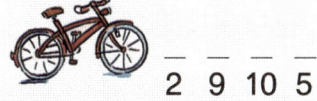

$\overline{2}$ $\overline{9}$ $\overline{10}$ $\overline{5}$

1=a	6=f	11=l	16=s
2=b	7=g	12=n	17=t
3=c	8=h	13=o	18=u
4=d	9=i	14=p	19=x
5=e	10=k	15=r	20=y

$\overline{14}$ $\overline{11}$ $\overline{1}$ $\overline{12}$ $\overline{5}$

$\overline{17}$ $\overline{1}$ $\overline{19}$ $\overline{9}$

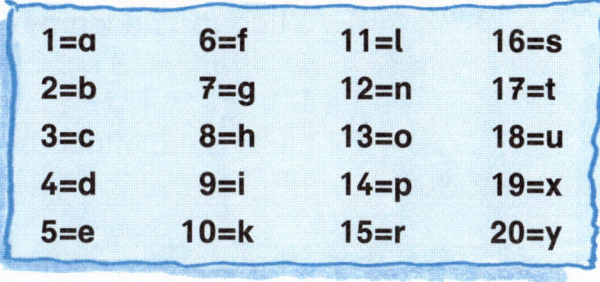

$\overline{18}$ $\overline{12}$ $\overline{4}$ $\overline{5}$ $\overline{15}$ $\overline{7}$ $\overline{15}$ $\overline{13}$ $\overline{18}$ $\overline{12}$ $\overline{4}$

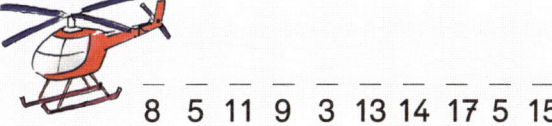

$\overline{11}$ $\overline{13}$ $\overline{15}$ $\overline{15}$ $\overline{20}$

$\overline{2}$ $\overline{13}$ $\overline{1}$ $\overline{17}$

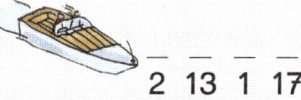

$\overline{8}$ $\overline{5}$ $\overline{11}$ $\overline{9}$ $\overline{3}$ $\overline{13}$ $\overline{14}$ $\overline{17}$ $\overline{5}$ $\overline{15}$

$\overline{17}$ $\overline{15}$ $\overline{1}$ $\overline{9}$ $\overline{12}$

$\overline{2}$ $\overline{18}$ $\overline{16}$

2. Sally likes to travel. Write.

| train | boat | car | plane |

 I go to London by _____ .

 I go to Scotland by _____ .

 I go to see my friend _____ .

 I go to see the Queen _____ .

3. Trace the lines and write.

Bob   Sandy   Tim   Ann

Bob is going by _____ .

Sandy is _____ .

Tim _____ .

Ann _____ .

 4. Number the traffic signs.

① **straight on**

② **turn left**

③ **turn right**

5. Where are the children going? Find the ways.

Lies die Wegbeschreibungen. Fahre mit Buntstift nach. In welche Geschäfte gehen die Kinder?

Tom: Turn left, go straight on, turn left again and then turn right.

Tom is going to the _____.

Susan: Go straight on, then turn right, go straight on and then turn right again.

Susan is _____.

Kim: Turn right, go straight on, turn left, then go straight on again and turn left again.

Kim _____.

Lies erst die Wegbeschreibung und fahre denWeg auf dem Plan nach. Verbinde dann die Frage mit der richtigen Wegbeschreibung.

6. Look at the map. Read and trace the way. Connect the answers and the questions. Fill in the missing words.

How do I get to the cinema, please?

Go straight on. Turn right into Baker Street. Turn left into River Street. The _____ is on the right.

How do I get to the book shop, please?

Turn left into Church Street. Turn right into School Street. Turn right again into Main Street. The _____ is on the left.

How do I get to the computer shop, please?

Turn left into Church Street. Go straight on. Turn right into School Street. Cross Main Street. The _____ is on the right.

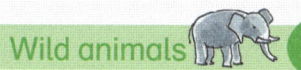

1. At the zoo you can see a lot of wild animals. ✔
   Do you know them? Write.

h _ p _ _

cr _ c _ _ i _ e

l _ o _

e _ e _ _ _ n _

gi _ a _ _ e

m _ _ ke _

k _ n _ a _ o _

z _ b _ _

elephant   lion   giraffe   monkey   hippo
zebra   crocodile   kangaroo

33

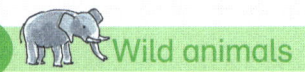
2. Match the legs to the animals. Draw lines and write. ✓

giraffe   elephant   bear   monkey   zebra   lion

3. What can the animals do? Write the correct answer. ✓

Yes, it can.   No, it can't.

Can a crocodile fly?   _____

Can a hippo swim?   _____

Can a snake jump?   _____

Can a monkey jump?   _____

Can a bear swim?   _____

Can a lion fly?   _____

Richtig oder falsch?
Schreibe die Antwort auf.

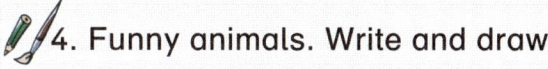 4. Funny animals. Write and draw.

head: giraffe

body: lion

legs: elephant

head: _____

body: _____

legs: _____

head: _____

body: _____

legs: _____

Now draw this animal:

The head is from a kangaroo.

The body is from a hippo.

The legs are from a zebra.

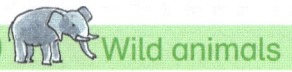

5. Find out their favourite animals. Read and write. ✔

Wir sollen die Lieblingstiere von Tim, Ben, Mary, Jenny und Sally herausfinden.

kangaroo

lion

koala   bear

snake

giraffe

hippo

elephant

crocodile   ZOO   zebra   monkey

Tim

My favourite animal is green. It has got a big mouth with sharp teeth. My favourite animal is a _____ .

Ben

My favourite animal is grey and has got a long nose.

My favourite animal is an _____ .

Mary

And my favourite animal is brown and likes bananas.

My _____ .

Jenny

My animal is brown and yellow and has got a long neck.

My _____ .

Sally

My favourite animal is brown and can jump.

My _____ .

36

6. Read the comic.

Sally and Koala at the zoo

1. Fill in. ✔

-ache

head	back
ear	tooth
stomach	

2. Fill in and draw lines. ✔

Sally's ear hurts. She has got an __earache__ .

Sally's tooth hurts. She has got a _____ .

Sally's back hurts. She has got a _____ .

Sally's head hurts. She has got a _____ .

Sally's stomach hurts. She has got a _____ .

| headache | earache | stomachache | backache | toothache |

 3. What's the matter? Read and fill in.

I have eaten
5 pizzas.

You have got a

_____ .

I have fallen
from a tree.

You have got a

_____ .

My nose is running.

You have got a

_____ .

My head feels hot.

You have got a

_____ .

You have got a

_____ .

I have carried
ten boxes of lollipops.

| cold | broken arm | backache | fever | stomachache |

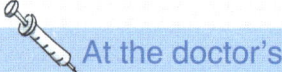

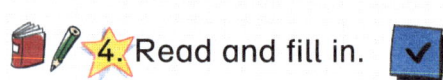 4. Read and fill in. ✓

Ben is sitting in the _____ .

The _____ comes in and says: "Next, please!"

It's Ben's turn. The _____ asks Ben: "What's

the matter?"

"I'm ill. I've got a _____ , I've got a

_____ and I think I've got a _____ , too.

I can't go to school today."

The _____ says: "Ben, you are not ill. Why can't

you go to school today?"

"We have got a math test today, Daddy."

| doctor (2x)   fever   nurse   headache |
| cold   waiting room |

5. Read the comic. **?**

A lollipop will help

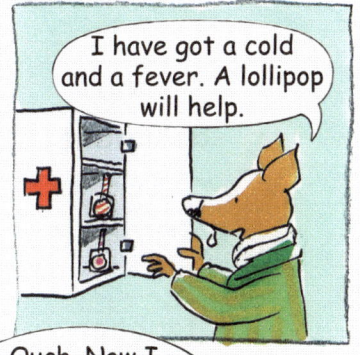

I have got a cold and a fever. A lollipop will help.

HA - HA -

TSCHII!

Ouch. Now I have got a headache, too. But a lollipop will help.

And now I have also got a backache. But a lollipop will help.

Oh, I think I had too many lollipops. I have got a stomach-ache...

DOCTOR

Poor Sally. A lollipop will help.

Oh no!

1. Guess the jobs. Write.

 Sally is a _____ .

 Sally _____ .

 Sally _____ .

 Sally is a _____ and

Koala is a _____ .

 Sally _____ .

 Sally is an _____ and

Koala is an _____ .

 Koala is a _____ .

 Sally is a _____ .

| shop assistant |
| hairdresser |
| teacher |
| doctor |
| policewoman/ policeman |
| actress/ actor |
| vet |
| football player |

2. My jobs at home. Draw lines and write. ☑

I have to ...

make ———————— the cat

feed ———————— my bed

help ———————— my room

do ———————— in the kitchen

walk ———————— in the garden

tidy ———————— the dog

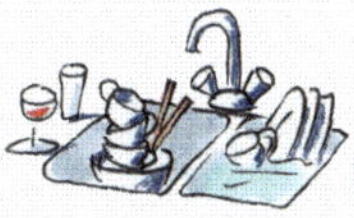

help ———————— my homework

I have to _make my bed._

I _____ .

_____ .

_____ .

_____ .

_____ .

_____ .

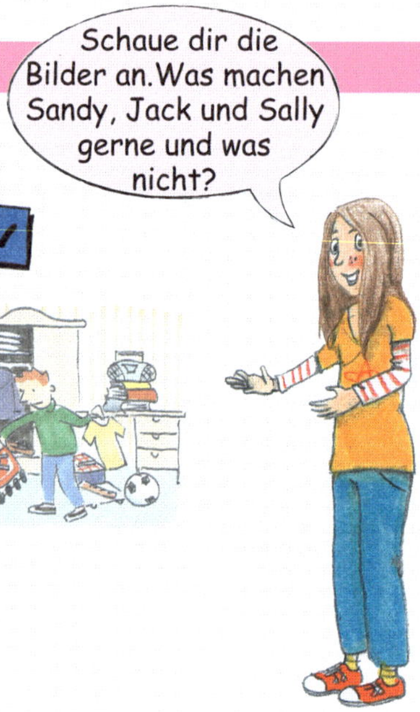

Schaue dir die Bilder an. Was machen Sandy, Jack und Sally gerne und was nicht?

3. Look at Sandy, Jack and Sally.
   Which jobs do they like and which not? Write. ✔

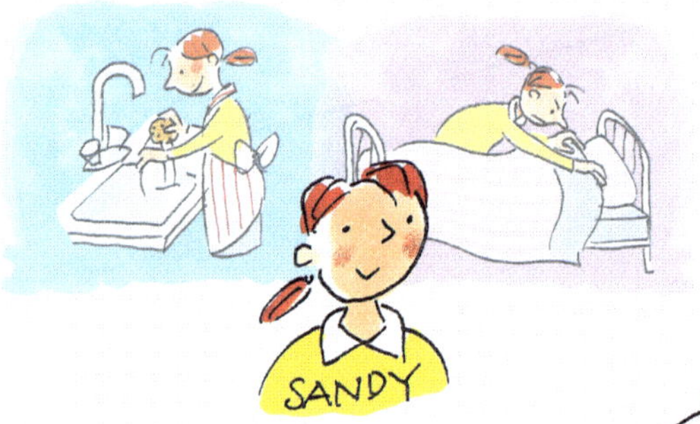

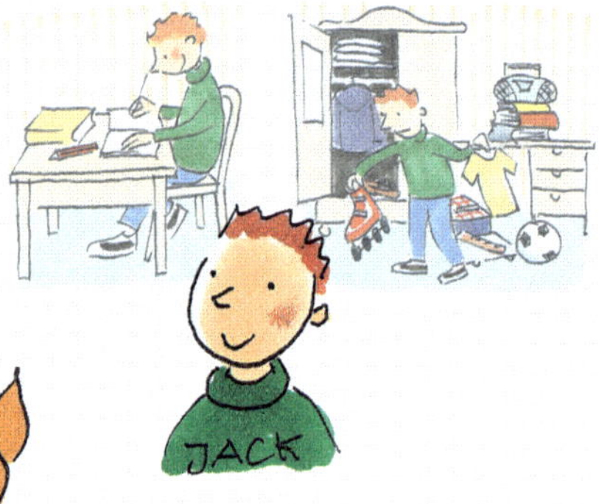

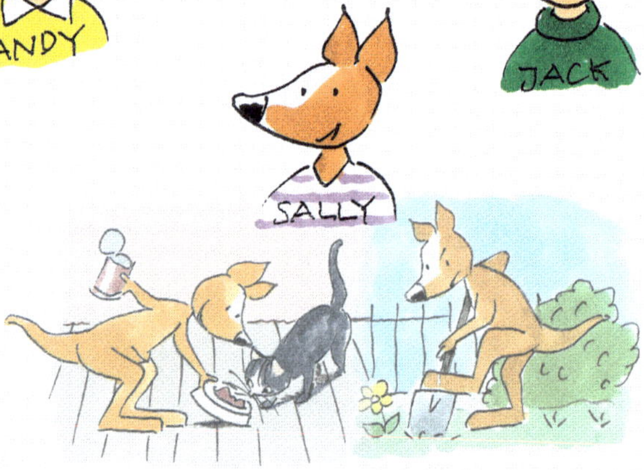

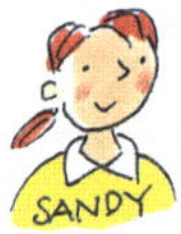

I like to _____ , but

I don't like to _____ .

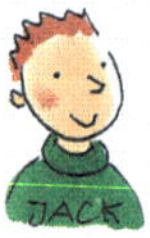

I like to _____ , but

I don't like to _____ .

_____ ,

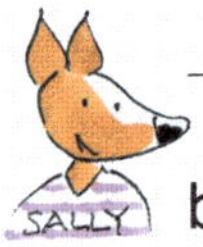

but _____ .

And what about you? Write.

I _____ ,

but _____ .

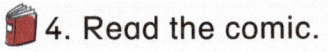 4. Read the comic.

Sally, what do you want to be?

Sally, what do you want to be?

I want to be a shop assistant.

The trousers are too small.

The shirt is too big.

No, I want to be a hairdresser.

I look horrible.

No, no, I want to be a policewoman.

Help!

TUUT!

I want to be a…, a…, a…

I just want to be a … happy kangaroo!!!

45

1. Where are the children from? Write. ✓

G r m e a n y   I'm from Germany.

S U A   I'm from the _____.

S i p a n   I'm _____.

G a r t e   B n a r i t i   _____.

F n e a c r   _____.

P n o a l d   _____.

T e r k y u   _____.

R s a s i u   _____.

l a y t l   _____.

**Turkey   Italy   USA   Russia   France   Great Britain
Spain   Germany   Poland**

 **2.** Guess the country. Read and write. ☑

 I love to eat baguette and croissants. I say "Bonjour!" and not "Hello!". The capital of my country is Paris.

I'm from _____ .

 The name of our flag is Union Jack. The capital of my country is London. We have a Queen.

I'm from _____ .

 I eat spaghetti almost every day. But I also like to eat pizza. The capital of my country is Rome.

I'm from _____ .

 The capital of my country is Berlin. I say "Hallo!".

I'm from _____ .

 I don't say "Hello!", I say "Merhaba!". A lot of people come to my country for their holidays.

The capital of my country is Ankara.

I'm from _____ .

Turkey   France   Germany   Italy   Great Britain

3. Read and fill in.

Are you from _____ 🇩🇪 ?

Yes, I am. Are you from _____ 🇩🇪 , too?

No, I'm not. I'm from _____ 🇮🇹 .

Are you from the _____ 🇺🇸 ?

No, _____ . I'm from _____ 🇪🇸 .

Hello, I'm from _____ 🇬🇧 . Are you

from _____ 🇬🇧 , too?

No, _____ . I'm from _____ 🇷🇺 .

Are you from _____ 🇹🇷 ?

Yes, _____ . Are you from _____ 🇪🇸 ?

No, _____ . I'm from _____ 🇵🇱 .

| USA | Spain | Poland | Russia | Germany | Turkey |
| Great Britain | Italy |

48

4. Read the comic. [?]

Sally's trip around the world

1. Find the flag of the USA. Circle. ☑

Wo hat sich die amerikanische Flagge versteckt?

2. Do you know these New York sights? Trace the lines. ☑ ?

Empire State Building   Brooklyn Bridge   Central Park   Statue of Liberty

3. Where's Sally? Draw lines and write.

Sally is…

in

in front of

behind

under

next to

on

   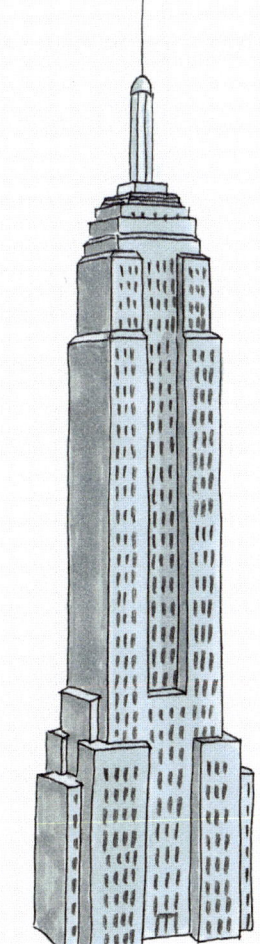

4. Circle the correct name of the USA.

the United Stars of America

the United States of America

the United Stripes of America

 5. Correct or wrong? Tick.

correct   wrong

The name of the flag of the USA is Union Jack.

Americans pay with dollars and cents.

New York is one of the biggest cities in the USA.

The Empire State Building is a small house.

Central Park is a big park in New York.

The Queen is the president of the USA.

The people in the USA speak English.

The capital of the USA is London.

The capital of the USA is Washington D.C.

Du weißt schon viel über die USA.
Was stimmt und was ist falsch?
Mache einen Haken.

eleven   twelve   thirteen   fourteen   fifteen   sixteen
seventeen   eighteen   nineteen   twenty   thirty   forty
fifty   sixty   seventy   eighty   ninety   one hundred

room: _ _ _ _ _ _ _

room: _ _ _ _ _ _

_ _ _ _ _

_ _ _ _ _

_ _ _ _ _

_ _ _ _ _

_ _ _ _ _ _

_ _ _ _ _

_ _ _ _ _

_ _ _ _ _

room: _ _ _ _ _

room: _ _ _ _ _ _ _   _ _ _ _ _ _

toilet   bathroom   living room   bedroom   kitchen
garage   garden   door   stairs   chair   table   bed
lamp   cupboard   shelves   desk   sofa

54

fish and chips
spaghetti
chicken salad
pizza
tomato
ham
ketchup
bread
mustard
lettuce
cucumber
cheese

carrot
soup
menu
sausage
with
mashed
potatoes

plate
knife
fork
spoon
to drink
to eat
sandwich

In the morning:

I get up at seven o'clock.

I have breakfast at
eight o'clock.

School starts at
nine o'clock.

In the afternoon:

I do my homework
at three o'clock.

What time is it?
It's four o'clock.

I play with my friends
at four o'clock.

In the evening / at night:

I go to bed and sleep
at nine o'clock.

skateboarding

riding a mountain bike

reading books

swimming

playing tennis

playing basketball

playing football

riding a horse

snowboarding

ice skating

inline skating

playing the piano

playing the guitar

supermarket   music shop   clothes shop
toy shop   sports shop   biscuits   just right
too big   shoe shop   too small   sweet shop
spinach   chocolate bars   book shop

bus   taxi   bike   car   underground   train   lorry   plane   helicopter   boat
straight on   turn right   turn left

koala   zebra   lion   snake   hippo   giraffe   elephant
monkey   crocodile   kangaroo   bear

headache   earache   stomachache   backache   broken arm
toothache   waiting room   nurse   doctor   cold   fever

61

Jobs

| shop assistant | hairdresser | teacher | doctor |
| policewoman/policeman | actress/actor | vet | football player |

Jobs at home

I...

feed the cat

help in the garden

make my bed

walk the dog

help in the kitchen

do my homework

tidy my room

Informationen für Eltern und Lehrkräfte

Englisch spielerisch üben mit den Englisch-Stars

Aufbau und Gestaltung der Englisch-Stars

Mit den Englisch-Stars üben und sichern die Kinder auf spielerische Weise den für die Grundschule wichtigen Wortschatz sowie ihr Lese- und Schreibvermögen. Abwechslungsreiche Übungsformen und ansprechende Illustrationen motivieren, Wörter und Strukturen vielfältig anzuwenden.

Das Känguru Sally ist dabei ständiger Begleiter. Die beiden deutschsprachigen Kinder Lisa und Max unterstützen mit Tipps und Hilfestellungen.

Die Englisch-Stars sind unterteilt in verschiedene Themenbereiche, die unabhängig voneinander bearbeitet werden können. Zusätzlich bieten sie im Anhang ein kleines Picture dictionary (Bildwörterbuch). Zu jedem Thema gibt es dort eine Seite, die den Wortschatz einführt. Daher ist es empfehlenswert, diese jeweils als Erstes zu bearbeiten.
Im Anschluss folgen vielfältige Übungen zur Wortschatzwiederholung und -sicherung sowie zur Sicherung des Lese- und Schreibvermögens, z.B. Zuordnungsaufgaben, Bilderrätsel und Dialoge. Lustige Comics mit Sally zeigen den Kindern, wie viel sie schon selbstständig lesen und verstehen können.
Eindeutige Aufgabenstellungen und Selbstkontrolle durch den Lösungsteil ermöglichen den Kindern, eigenständig mit den Englisch-Stars zu arbeiten.

Für jede Seite im Picture dictionary, nach jedem Thema, für jeden gelesenen Comic und für besonders schwierige Aufgaben (Sternchenaufgaben) dürfen sich die Kinder mit einem Sternchen-Aufkleber belohnen. Als besonderer Anreiz ergeben die Sterne am Ende des Heftes ein Gesamtbild.

Die Englisch-Stars dienen der spielerischen und zwanglosen Auseinandersetzung mit Englisch und fördern die Freude am Erlernen der Fremdsprache.

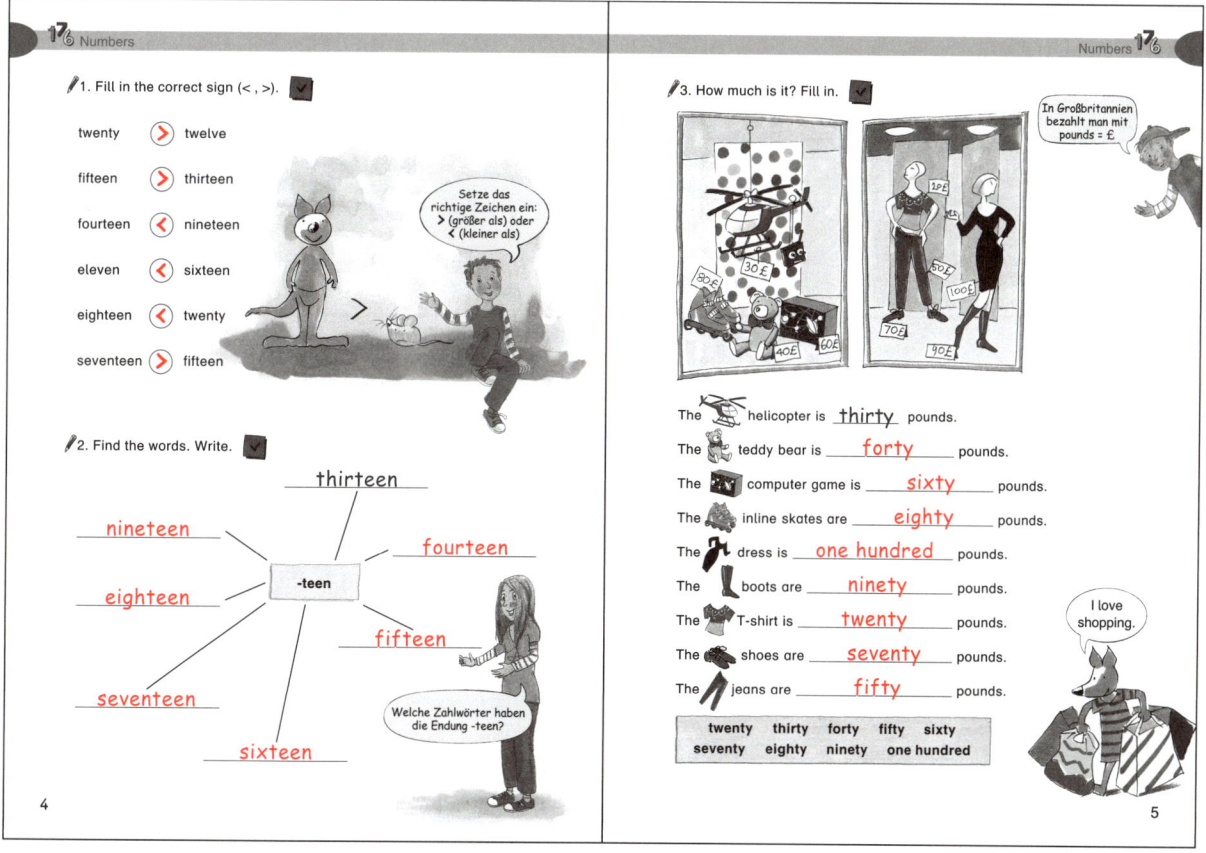

Lösungen

1. Find the words and circle them. Fill in. ✓

Suche die Wörter senkrecht und waagrecht. Kreise ein. Trage dann unten die durcheinandergeratenen Wörter richtig ein.

k	o	b	a	t	h	r	o	o	m
z	g	c	d	o	o	r	z	k	l
g	a	u	h	i	y	t	i	w	r
f	r	e	a	l	b	g	y	w	b
n	d	h	r	e	v	w	e	i	e
a	e	k	i	t	c	h	e	n	d
z	n	d	e	s	h	f	x	d	r
h	k	g	a	r	a	g	e	o	o
j	s	t	a	i	r	s	b	w	o
l	i	v	i	n	g	r	o	o	m

living room	toilet
bedroom	stairs
kitchen	bathroom
garden	window
garage	door

Lucy is cooking in the **ikcehtn** _kitchen_ .

Mum is watching TV in the **vngiil mroo** _living room_ .

The car is in the **ggraae** _garage_ .

Dad is sleeping in the **dbrmooe** _bedroom_ .

Kevin is playing in the **nraged** _garden_ .

Emma is taking a bath in the **ohatobmr** _bathroom_ .

Sally is reading on the **otielt** _toilet_ .

6

2. What is it? Complete and draw lines. ✓

Was hat sich hinter den Bildausschnitten versteckt? Vervollständige erst die Wörter und verbinde dann mit dem richtigen Bild.

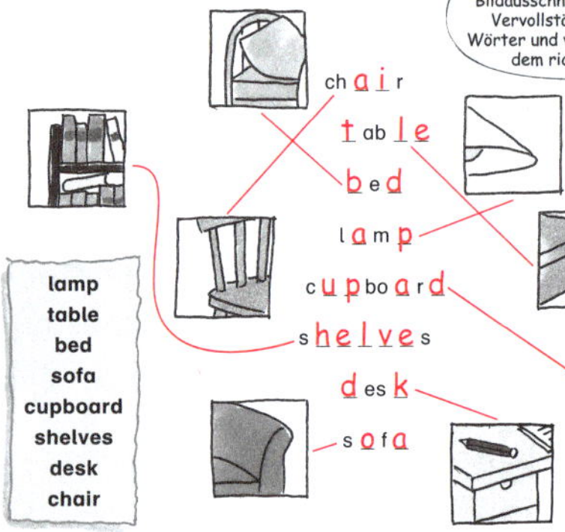

ch**a**i**r**
tab**le**
be**d**
la**p**
cu**pb**o**ard**
sh**e**l**ve**s
des**k**
s**ofa**

| lamp |
| table |
| bed |
| sofa |
| cupboard |
| shelves |
| desk |
| chair |

3. Find the furniture and colour the fields brown. What can you see? ✓

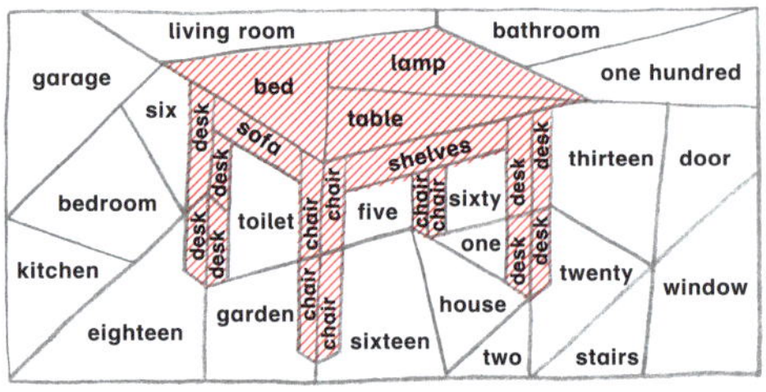

	living room		bathroom	
garage		lamp		one hundred
	six	bed		
		sofa	table	thirteen	door
			shelves	
bedroom			sixty	five	
		toilet		one	twenty	window
kitchen				house	
eighteen		garden	sixteen	two	stairs

I can see a _table_ .

7

4. Describe the rooms. Fill in. ✓

Was gibt es alles in den verschiedenen Räumen zu sehen? Schreibe auf. Passe bei cupboard und cupboards auf.

In the _bedroom_ there's a _bed_ and two _cupboards_ .

| bedroom |
| kitchen |
| living room |

In the _living room_ there's a _sofa_ , a _table_ , a _lamp_ and three _shelves_ .

shelves	cupboards
lamp	bed
chairs	cupboard
table (2x)	sofa

In the _kitchen_ there's a _table_ with four _chairs_ and a _cupboard_ .

8

5. Crazy rooms. Read and number. ✓

Welche Beschreibung passt zu welchem Zimmer?

③ My room is purple. I've got a table with three chairs and a pink bed. I've also got a pink toilet and a small garden.

① My room has got a small bed, a small desk with a chair and two big shelves.

② I live in a very dark room. In my room there's a red sofa and a black cupboard. I don't like lamps.

9

At home

6. Read the comic. ?

Is there a room for me?

My room is too small. I need a new home.

I have to find a new home. Let's see where I can live.

Where do you live? Is there a room for me?

This is my home. It's too small for two people, sorry.

Where do you live? Is there a room for me?

My home is down there. It's too dark for you.

Where do you live? Is there a room for me?

My home is a big house with three big bedrooms. One for Mum and Dad, one for me and one for you. Come and live with me.

That's great. Thank you.

10

Let's have lunch

1. Find the words. Draw lines and write. ✓

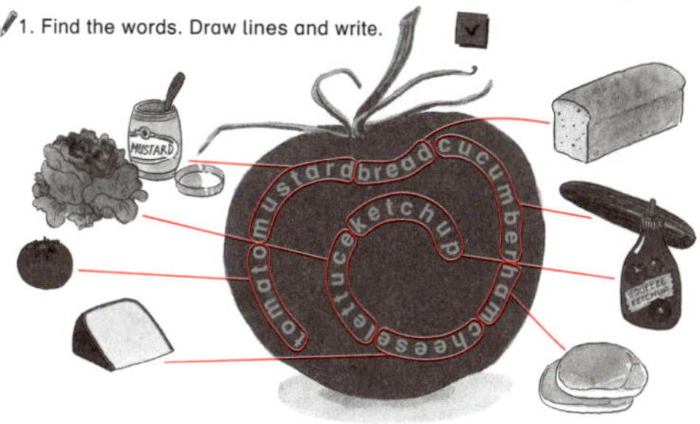

tomato, mustard, bread, cucumber, ham, cheese, lettuce, ketchup

| mustard | lettuce | ham | cheese | bread | ketchup |
| tomato | cucumber |

2. Read and draw lines. ✓

I like a sandwich with tomatoes, cheese and cucumbers.

I like a sandwich with mustard, ham, lettuce and ketchup.

I like a sandwich with ham, cheese and lettuce.

11

Let's have lunch

3. What is it? Read and write. ✓

It's brown and soft. — It's _bread_.

It's green and long. — It's a _cucumber_.

It's yellow and a mouse likes it. — It's _cheese_.

It's yellow, but it's not cheese. — It's _mustard_.

It's green and has got leaves. — It's _lettuce_.

It's pink and part of an animal. — It's _ham_.

It's red and looks like a small ball. — It's a _tomato_.

It's red, but it's not a tomato. — It's _ketchup_.

| bread | tomato | cheese | ham | cucumber | ketchup |
| mustard | lettuce |

4. Write and draw lines. ✓

Achtung bei der Mehrzahl von knife: one knife _aber_ two kni_ves_

p l a t e

f o r k

k n i f e

s p o o n

plate
knife
fork
spoon

12

Let's have lunch

5. What's on the menu? Number and write. ✓

④ ③ ①
⑥ ⑤ ②

1. carrot soup	£3.00	4. fish and chips	£5.00
2. pizza	£5.00	5. sausage with mashed
3. spaghetti	£5.50	potatoes	£7.50
		6. chicken salad	£4.50

6. Do you know what the children want? Write. ✓

Die bestellen ja alles völlig verdreht! Schreibe es richtig auf.

I'd like spaghetti soup and a carrot.

I'd like spaghetti and a carrot soup

I'd like a fish salad and chicken and chips.

I'd like a chicken salad and fish and chips

I'd like a mashed carrot and a sausage soup with potatoes.

I'd like a carrot soup and a sausage with mashed potatoes

13

Lösungen

7. Complete the dialogue. Write.

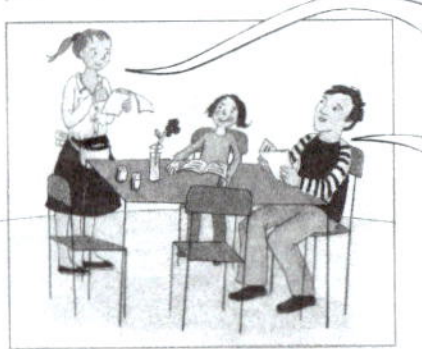

What would you like to __eat__?

We'd like a 🌭 __sausage with mashed potatoes__ and a 🍕 __pizza__, please.

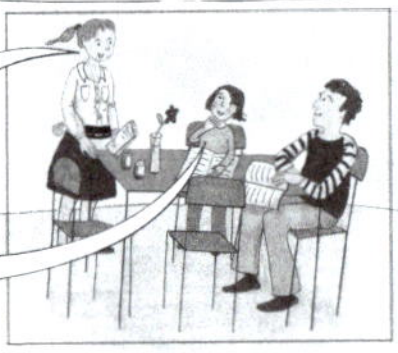

Would you like something to __drink__, too?

We'd like a 🍾 __coke__ and a 🥤 __lemonade__, please.

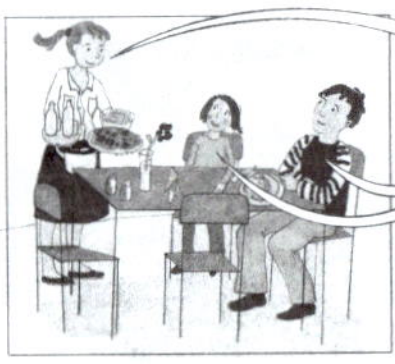

Here you are.

__Thank you__.

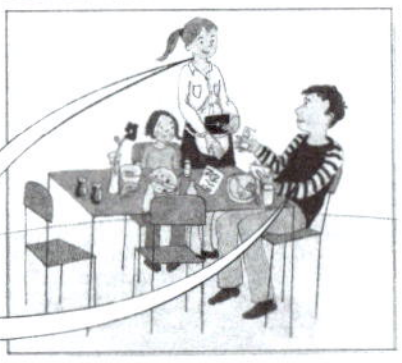

That's twenty pounds.

__Here you are__

pizza	drink	eat	Here you are	Thank you
coke	lemonade	sausage with mashed potatoes		

8. Read the comic.

Sally likes lollipops

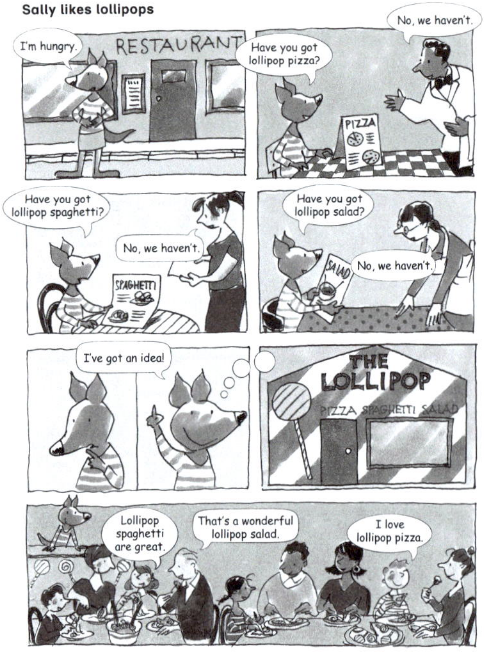

I'm hungry. — RESTAURANT

Have you got lollipop pizza?

No, we haven't.

Have you got lollipop spaghetti?

No, we haven't.

Have you got lollipop salad?

No, we haven't.

I've got an idea!

THE LOLLIPOP
PIZZA SPAGHETTI SALAD

Lollipop spaghetti are great.

That's a wonderful lollipop salad.

I love lollipop pizza.

14

15

Zeichne die Uhrzeiger richtig ein und spure dann die Sätze nach.

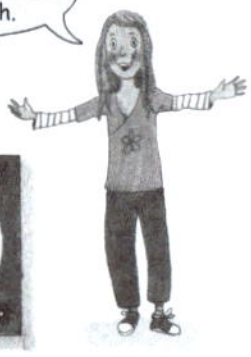

1. Draw the clock's hands and write.

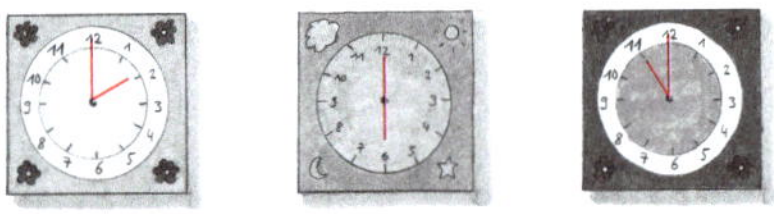

It's
two o'clock.

It's
six o'clock.

It's
eleven o'clock.

2. What time is it? Write.

nine	eight
five	three
twelve	

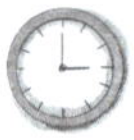

It's three o'clock.

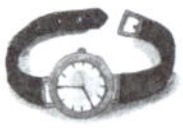

It's eight o'clock.

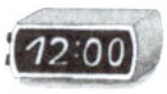

It's twelve o'clock.

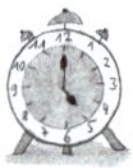

It's five o'clock.

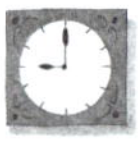

It's nine o'clock.

3. Write and draw lines.

Lucy's day

get up   play with my friends
do my homework   have breakfast
go to bed and sleep   go to school

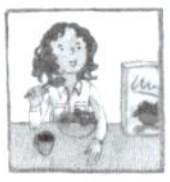

I have breakfast

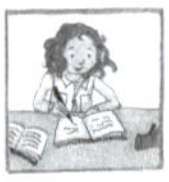

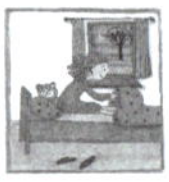

I __do my homework__

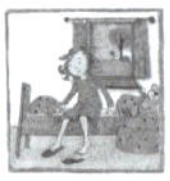

I __get up__

in the morning.

in the afternoon.

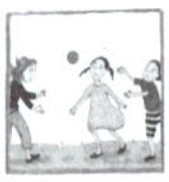

I __play with my friends__

in the evening / at night.

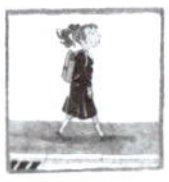

I __go to bed and sleep__

I __go to school__

16

17

My day

4. An interview. Read and fill in. ✔

Hello, Ben.

Hello, _____ (your name).

When do you get up?

I get up at _seven_ o'clock.

When do you start school?

I start _school at nine o'clock_

When do you do your homework?

I do my _homework at four o'clock_

When do you play with your friends?

I play with my _friends at five o'clock_

When do you go to bed and sleep?

I go _to bed and sleep at nine o'clock_

Thank you for the interview. Goodbye.

You're welcome. Bye.

18

My day

5. Read the comic. ?

Time for breakfast?

19

Hobbies and sports

1. Trace the lines and write. ✔

Eric likes **riding a mountain bike.**
John likes **reading books.**
Kim likes **swimming.**
Judy likes **riding a horse.**
Nick likes **playing football.**
Andy likes **snowboarding.**
Lucy likes **playing the piano.**
Emma likes **ice skating.**
Martha likes **playing the guitar.**

20

Hobbies and sports

2. Guess the hobby. Read and write. ✔

My favourite hobby is playing an instrument. My instrument is very big. I can play a lot of songs on it.

In summer it's the perfect hobby. I jump into the water and I'm happy. **Betty**

For my hobby I sit on an animal. The animal likes to eat grass, apples and carrots. It's a big animal. **David**

Sam

Ron

I can do my favourite hobby wherever I want. I only need a book.

Linda

Kathy

For my hobby I need a ball. I hit the ball with my feet.

I do my hobby in winter. I go to the mountains. I love snow.

Linda's hobby is _snowboarding_.
Ron's _hobby is riding a horse_
Betty's _hobby is swimming_
Sam's _hobby is playing the piano_
Kathy's _hobby is playing football_
David's _hobby is reading books_

| snowboarding | reading books | riding a horse |
| swimming | playing the piano | playing football |

21

Lösungen

3. Look at the pictures and write. ✓

Jane   Harry   Bill

Can Jane play tennis? — Yes, she can.
Can Harry play football? — No, he can't.
Can Jane ice skate? — No, she can't.
Can Bill ride a horse? — Yes, he can.
Can Harry play tennis? — No, he can't.
Can Jane play the guitar? — Yes, she can.
Can Bill play basketball? — No, he can't.
Can Harry swim? — Yes, he can.
Can Bill ride a skateboard? — Yes, he can.

Denke daran: Verwende bei Jungen he, bei Mädchen she.

And what can you do?

I can _____

22

Read and fill in. ✓

Hello. What's your name?

Hi. My __name__ is Tom. __What's__ your name?

__My name__ is Helen.
What's your favourite hobby?

My favourite __hobby__ is __playing football__ .
What's your __favourite hobby__ ?

I like __playing football__ , too.
Let's play together!

Good idea! Let's go!

And I like playing football, too.

23

1. At the shopping centre. Write. ✓

SUPERMARKET   MUSIC SHOP   CLOTHES SHOP   SWEET SHOP

TOY SHOP   BOOK SHOP   SPORTS SHOP   SHOE SHOP

In the supermarket I can buy __orange juice__
In the music shop I __can buy CDs__
__In the clothes shop I can buy pullovers__
__In the sweet shop I can buy lollipops__
__In the toy shop I can buy teddy bears__
__In the book shop I can buy books__
__In the sports shop I can buy inline skates__
__In the shoe shop I can buy shoes__

| orange juice | CDs | books | shoes | lollipops |
| pullovers | inline skates | teddy bears | | |

24

2. In the clothes shop. Write. ✓

Are the clothes just right?

No, the jacket is too big.

Yes, the dress is just right.

No, the pullover is too small .

No, the shoes are too big .

Yes, the skirt is just right .

| too big | too small | just right | pullover | dress |
| shoes | skirt | jacket | | |

25

Page 26

3. In the supermarket. Whose shopping basket is it?
Add the missing things to the list. ✓

Wem gehört welcher Einkaufskorb? Ergänze die fehlenden Dinge.

George

Andy

Olivia

Sarah

Sarah
coffee, eggs, cherries, lemonade, spinach, jam

George
bananas, milk, honey, biscuits, water, apple juice

Andy
pineapple, ham, butter, cornflakes, milk, cheese, tea, rolls

Olivia
bread, coke, oranges, chocolate bars, eggs, bacon

butter	honey	lemonade	bacon	cherries	tea	spinach
jam	milk	oranges	water	chocolate bars	eggs	rolls
cheese	apple juice	cornflakes	biscuits			

Page 27

4. In the sports shop. Read and number. ✓

It's £30.   **4**

Here you are. Goodbye.

Thank you. Bye.

Here are the skateboards. Do you like the colour?   **2**

No, sorry. I don't like red.

Hello. Can I help you?   **1**

Hello. I'd like a new skateboard.

Do you like the green skateboard?   **3**

It's perfect. Green is my favourite colour!

Page 28

5. Read the comic. **?**

Sally goes shopping

Sally, can you please go to the supermarket for me? Here is the shopping list.

Okay Mum. Bye.

spinach
eggs
potatoes
bread
butter
cheese

I don't like spinach and potatoes.

bread
eggs
cheese
potatoes
butter
spinach

But I like chocolate, apples, strawberries and lemonade.

Oh no, Sally. And what do we eat for dinner now?

Oh Mum! This dinner is fantastic.

Page 29

1. Find the correct word. Write. ✓

c a r
3 1 15

b i k e
2 9 10 5

p l a n e
14 11 1 12 5

t a x i
17 1 19 9

u n d e r g r o u n d
18 12 4 5 15 7 15 13 18 12 4

l o r r y
11 13 15 15 20

b o a t
2 13 1 17

h e l i c o p t e r
8 5 11 9 3 13 14 17 5 15

t r a i n
17 15 1 9 12

b u s
2 18 16

1=a	6=f	11=l	16=s
2=b	7=g	12=n	17=t
3=c	8=h	13=o	18=u
4=d	9=i	14=p	19=x
5=e	10=k	15=r	20=y

Lösungen

2. Sally likes to travel. Write.

train boat car plane

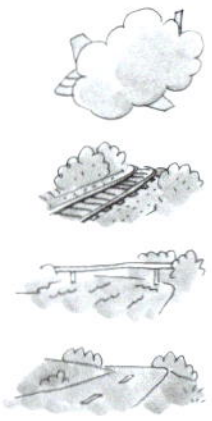

I go to London by plane.

I go to Scotland by train.

I go to see my friend by boat.

I go to see the Queen by car.

3. Trace the lines and write.

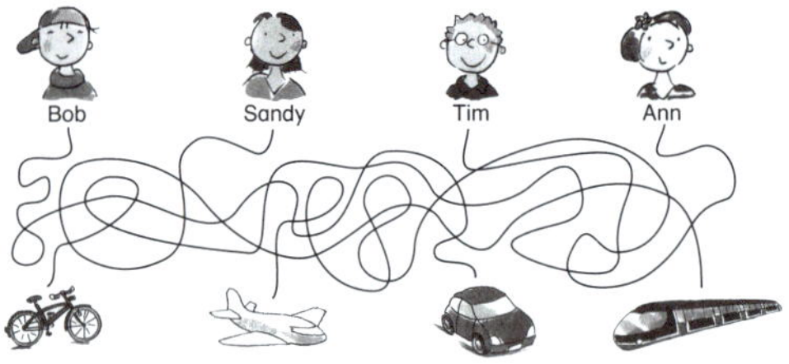

Bob
Sandy
Tim
Ann

Bob is going by car.

Sandy is going by train.

Tim is going by bike.

Ann is going by plane.

4. Number the traffic signs.

1. **straight on**
2. **turn left**
3. **turn right**

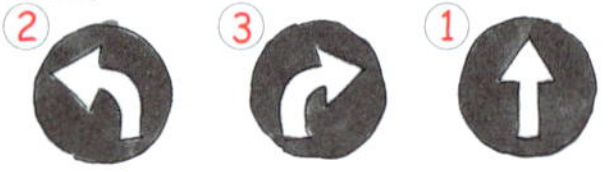

2
3
1

5. Where are the children going? Find the ways.

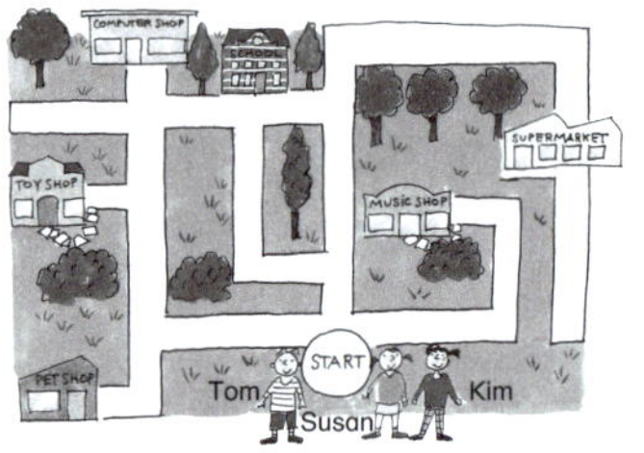

COMPUTER SHOP
TOY SHOP
SUPERMARKET
MUSIC SHOP
PET SHOP
START
Tom
Susan
Kim

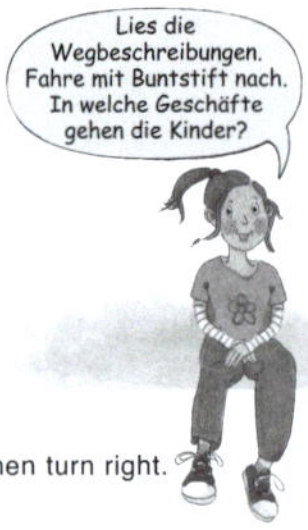

Lies die Wegbeschreibungen. Fahre mit Buntstift nach. In welche Geschäfte gehen die Kinder?

Tom: Turn left, go straight on, turn left again and then turn right.

Tom is going to the pet shop.

Susan: Go straight on, then turn right, go straight on and then turn right again.

Susan is going to the supermarket.

Kim: Turn right, go straight on, turn left, then go straight on again and turn left again.

Kim is going to the music shop.

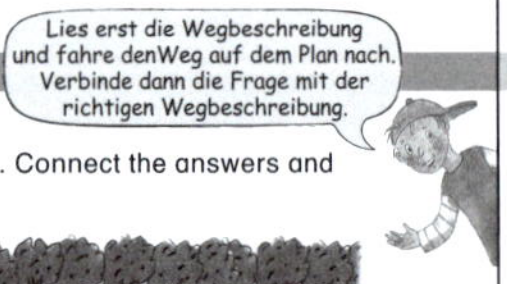

Lies erst die Wegbeschreibung und fahre den Weg auf dem Plan nach. Verbinde dann die Frage mit der richtigen Wegbeschreibung.

6. Look at the map. Read and trace the way. Connect the answers and the questions. Fill in the missing words.

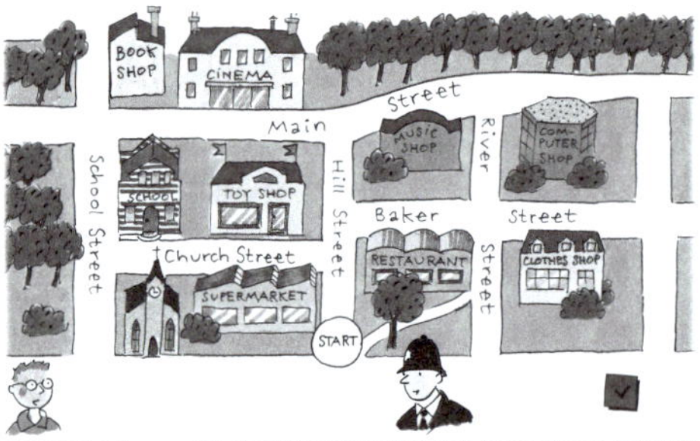

BOOK SHOP
CINEMA
Main Street
MUSIC SHOP
River Street
COMPUTER SHOP
School Street
SCHOOL
TOY SHOP
Hill Street
Baker Street
Church Street
RESTAURANT
CLOTHES SHOP
SUPERMARKET
START

How do I get to the cinema, please? — Go straight on. Turn right into Baker Street. Turn left into River Street. The computer shop is on the right.

How do I get to the book shop, please? — Turn left into Church Street. Turn right into School Street. Turn right again into Main Street. The cinema is on the left.

How do I get to the computer shop, please? — Turn left into Church Street. Go straight on. Turn right into School Street. Cross Main Street. The book shop is on the right.

1. At the zoo you can see a lot of wild animals. Do you know them? Write.

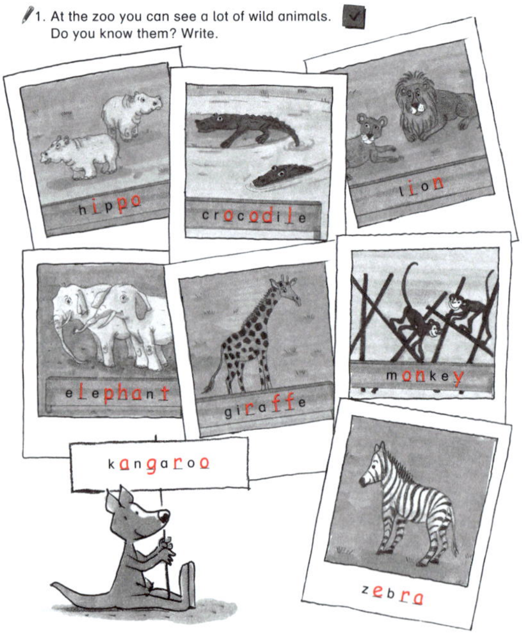

hippo
crocodile
lion
elephant
giraffe
monkey
kangaroo
zebra

elephant lion giraffe monkey hippo zebra crocodile kangaroo

---

2. Match the legs to the animals. Draw lines and write. ✓

giraffe   elephant   bear   monkey   zebra   lion

3. What can the animals do? Write the correct answer. ✓

| Yes, it can.   No, it can't. |

Can a crocodile fly?   No, it can't.
Can a hippo swim?   Yes, it can.
Can a snake jump?   No, it can't.
Can a monkey jump?   Yes, it can.
Can a bear swim?   Yes, it can.
Can a lion fly?   No, it can't.

Richtig oder falsch?
Schreibe die Antwort auf.

34

---

4. Funny animals. Write and draw. ✓

head: giraffe
body: lion
legs: elephant

head: _koala_
body: _snake_
legs: _kangaroo_

head: _bear_
body: _monkey_
legs: _crocodile_

Kopf: Känguru
Körper: Nilpferd
Beine: Zebra

Now draw this animal:

The head is from a kangaroo.
The body is from a hippo.
The legs are from a zebra.

35

---

5. Find out their favourite animals. Read and write. ✓

Wir sollen die
Lieblingstiere von
Tim, Ben, Mary,
Jenny und Sally
herausfinden.

kangaroo
koala   bear   lion
snake   giraffe
hippo   elephant
crocodile   zebra
ZOO   monkey

Tim My favourite animal is green. It has got a big mouth with sharp
teeth. My favourite animal is a _crocodile_ .

Ben My favourite animal is grey and has got a long nose.
My favourite animal is an _elephant_ .

Mary And my favourite animal is brown and likes bananas.
My _favourite animal is a monkey_ .

Jenny My animal is brown and yellow and has got a long neck.
My _favourite animal is a giraffe_ .

Sally My favourite animal is brown and can jump.
My _favourite animal is a kangaroo_ . ☆

36

---

6. Read the comic. ?

Sally and Koala at the zoo

37

Lösungen

1. Fill in. ✔

b a c k — -ache — **e a r**

t o o t h

s t o m a c h

h e a d

head	back
ear	tooth
stomach	

2. Fill in and draw lines. ✔

Sally's ear hurts. She has got an __earache__ .

Sally's tooth hurts. She has got a __toothache__ .

Sally's back hurts. She has got a __backache__ .

Sally's head hurts. She has got a __headache__ .

Sally's stomach hurts. She has got a __stomachache__ .

| headache | earache | stomachache | backache | toothache |

3. What's the matter? Read and fill in. ✔

I have eaten 5 pizzas. — You have got a __stomachache__ .

I have fallen from a tree. — You have got a __broken arm__ .

My nose is running. — You have got a __cold__ .

My head feels hot. — You have got a __fever__ .

I have carried ten boxes of lollipops. — You have got a __backache__ .

| cold | broken arm | backache | fever | stomachache |

4. Read and fill in. ✔

Ben is sitting in the __waiting room__ .

The __nurse__ comes in and says: "Next, please!"

It's Ben's turn. The __doctor__ asks Ben: "What's the matter?"

"I'm ill. I've got a __headache__ , I've got a __fever__ and I think I've got a __cold__ , too. I can't go to school today."

The __doctor__ says: "Ben, you are not ill. Why can't you go to school today?"

"We have got a math test today, Daddy."

| doctor (2x) | fever | nurse | headache |
| cold | waiting room | | |

5. Read the comic. ?

A lollipop will help

Lösungen

Jobs

1. Guess the jobs. Write. ✓

Sally is a **hairdresser**.

Sally **is a doctor**.

Sally **is a teacher**.

Sally is a **policewoman** and Koala is a **policeman**.

Sally **is a shop assistant**.

Sally is an **actress** and Koala is an **actor**.

Koala is a **vet**.

Sally is a **football player**.

shop assistant
hairdresser
teacher
doctor
policewoman/ policeman
actress/ actor
vet
football player

Jobs

2. My jobs at home. Draw lines and write. ✓

I have to ...

make —— my bed
feed —— the cat
help —— in the garden
do —— my homework
walk —— the dog
tidy —— my room
help —— in the kitchen

I have to **make my bed.**

I **have to feed the cat**.

I have to help in the garden.

I have to do my homework.

I have to walk the dog.

I have to tidy my room.

I have to help in the kitchen.

42   43

Jobs

3. Look at Sandy, Jack and Sally. Which jobs do they like and which not? Write. ✓

Schaue dir die Bilder an. Was machen Sandy, Jack und Sally gerne und was nicht?

I like to **help in the kitchen**, but
I don't like to **make my bed**.

I like to **do my homework**, but
I don't like to **clean my room**.

I like to feed the cat,
but **I don't like to help in the garden**.

And what about you? Write.

I _____ ,
but _____ .

Jobs

4. Read the comic. ❓

Sally, what do you want to be?

Sally, what do you want to be?

I want to be a shop assistant.

The trousers are too small.

The shirt is too big.

No, I want to be a hairdresser.

I look horrible.

No, no, I want to be a policewoman.

Help!   TUUT!

I want to be a..., a..., a...

I just want to be a ... happy kangaroo!!!

44   45

Lösungen

1. Where are the children from? Write. ✓

G r m e a n y — I'm from Germany.

S U A — I'm from the USA.

S i p a n — I'm from Spain.

G a r t e B n a r i t i — I'm from Great Britain.

F n e a c r — I'm from France.

P n o a l d — I'm from Poland.

T e r k y u — I'm from Turkey.

R s a s i u — I'm from Russia.

l a y t l — I'm from Italy.

| Turkey | Italy | USA | Russia | France | Great Britain |
| Spain | Germany | Poland | | | |

46

2. Guess the country. Read and write. ✓

I love to eat baguette and croissants. I say "Bonjour!" and not "Hello!". The capital of my country is Paris.

I'm from **France**.

The name of our flag is Union Jack. The capital of my country is London. We have a Queen.

I'm from **Great Britain**.

I eat spaghetti almost every day. But I also like to eat pizza. The capital of my country is Rome.

I'm from **Italy**.

The capital of my country is Berlin. I say "Hallo!".

I'm from **Germany**.

I don't say "Hello!", I say "Merhaba!". A lot of people come to my country for their holidays. The capital of my country is Ankara.

I'm from **Turkey**.

| Turkey | France | Germany | Italy | Great Britain |

47

3. Read and fill in. ✓

Are you from **Germany** ?

Yes, I am. Are you from **Germany** , too?

No, I'm not. I'm from **Italy** .

Are you from the **USA** ?

No, **I'm not** . I'm from **Spain** .

Hello, I'm from **Great Britain** . Are you from **Great Britain** , too?

No, **I'm not** . I'm from **Russia** .

Are you from **Turkey** ?

Yes, **I am** . Are you from **Spain** ?

No, **I'm not** . I'm from **Poland** .

| USA | Spain | Poland | Russia | Germany | Turkey |
| Great Britain | Italy | | | | |

48

4. Read the comic. ?

Sally's trip around the world

49

Lösungen

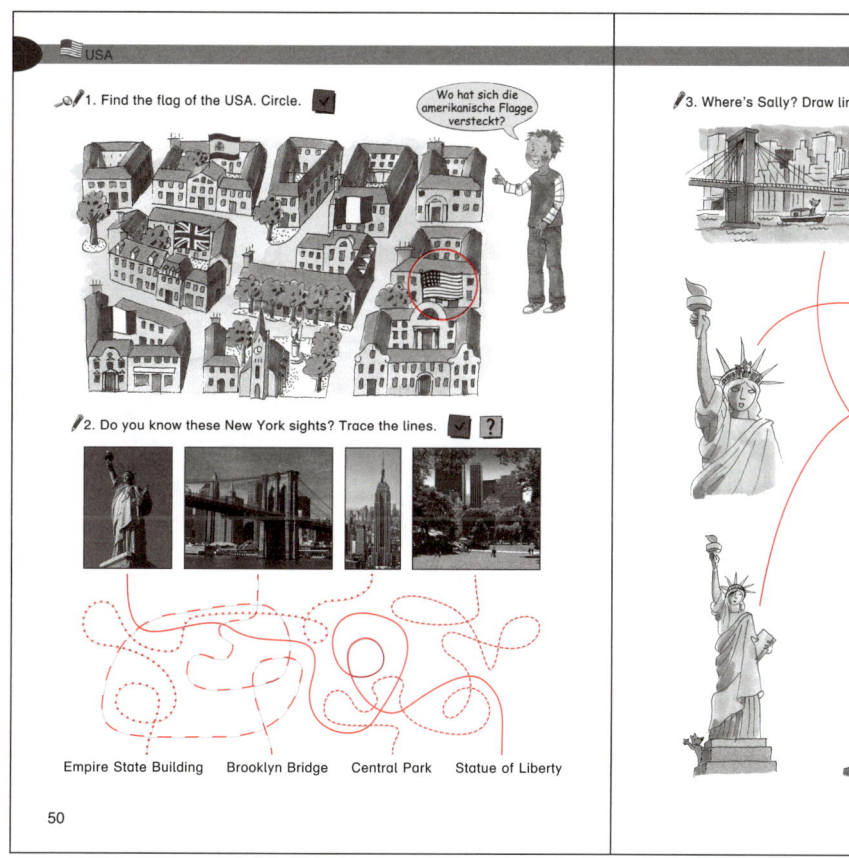

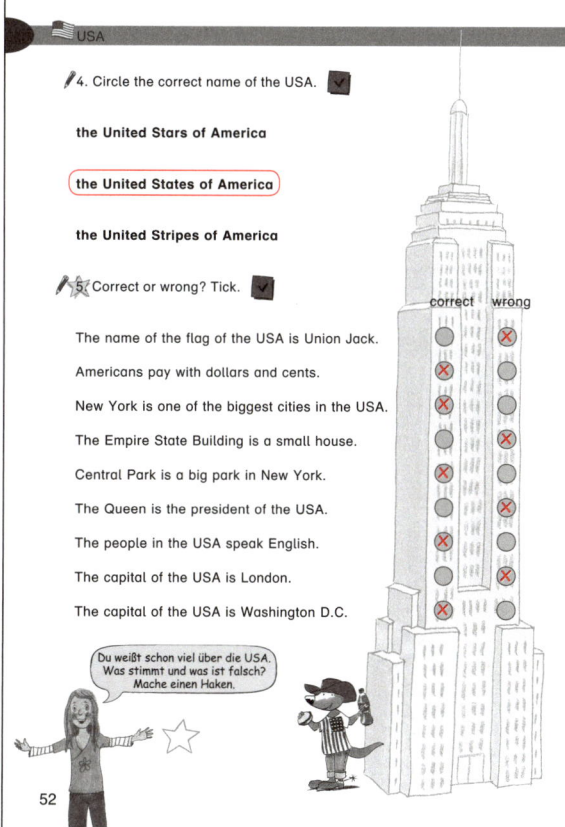

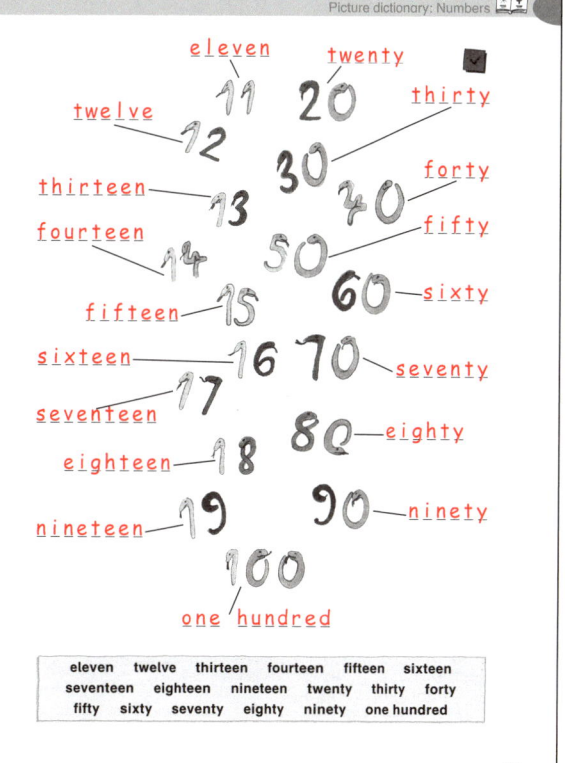

Lösungen

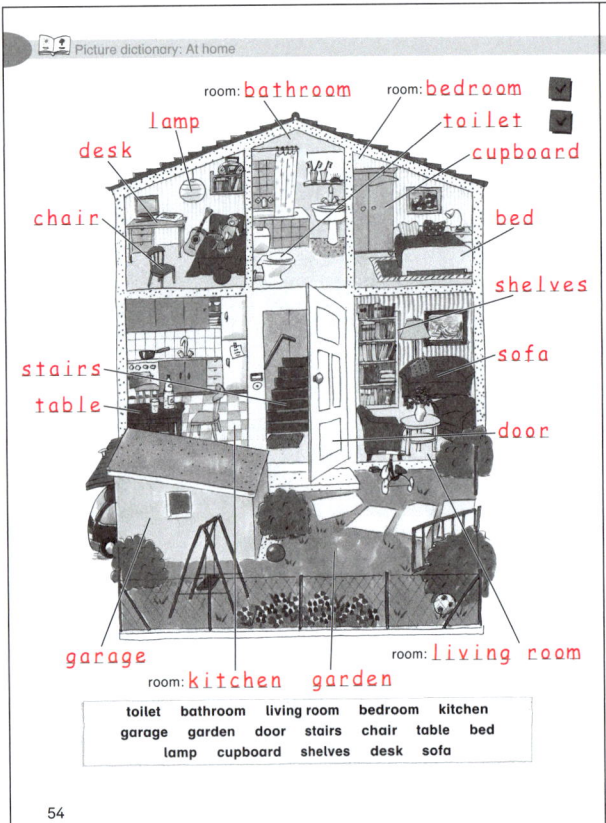

room: **bathroom**   room: **bedroom** ✓

lamp
toilet ✓
desk
cupboard
chair
bed
shelves
stairs
sofa
table
door
garage
room: **living room**
room: **kitchen**   garden

toilet	bathroom	living room	bedroom	kitchen
garage	garden	door	stairs	chair	table	bed
lamp	cupboard	shelves	desk	sofa

54

tomato   ham   ketchup   bread   mustard   lettuce   cucumber   cheese   sandwich
pizza   to eat
chicken salad   to drink
spoon
spaghetti   fork
knife
fish and chips   plate
carrot soup   menu   sausage with mashed potatoes

55

In the morning:

I get up at seven o'clock.

I have breakfast at eight o'clock.

School starts at nine o'clock.

In the afternoon:

I do my homework at three o'clock.

I play with my friends at four o'clock.

What time is it?
It's four o'clock.

In the evening / at night:

I go to bed and sleep at nine o'clock.

56

skateboarding
riding a mountain bike   reading books   swimming
playing tennis
playing basketball   playing football
snowboarding   ice skating
riding a horse
inline skating   playing the piano   playing the guitar

57

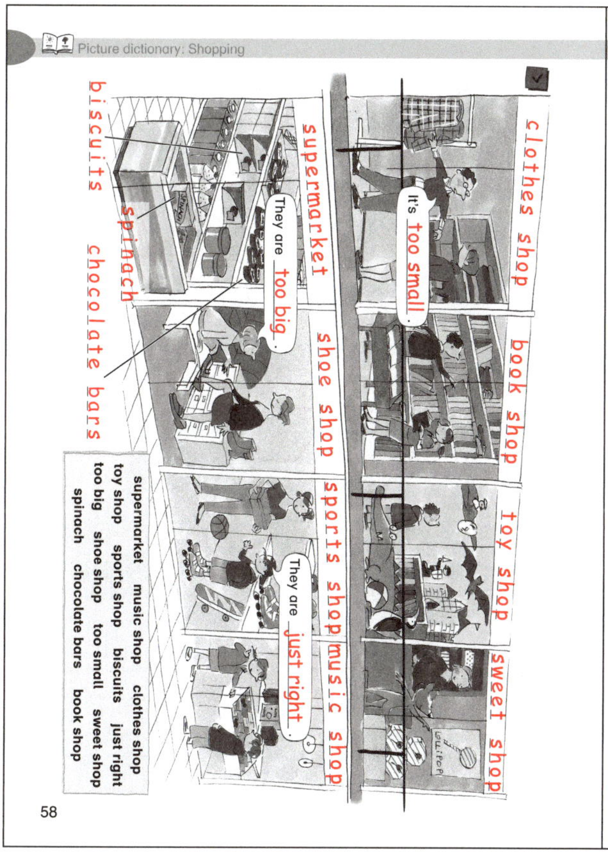
Picture dictionary: Shopping
clothes shop
book shop
toy shop
sweet shop
supermarket
shoe shop
sports shop
music shop
It's too small.
They are too big.
They are just right.
biscuits
spinach
chocolate bars
supermarket music shop clothes shop
toy shop sports shop biscuits just right
too big shoe shop too small sweet shop
spinach chocolate bars book shop
58

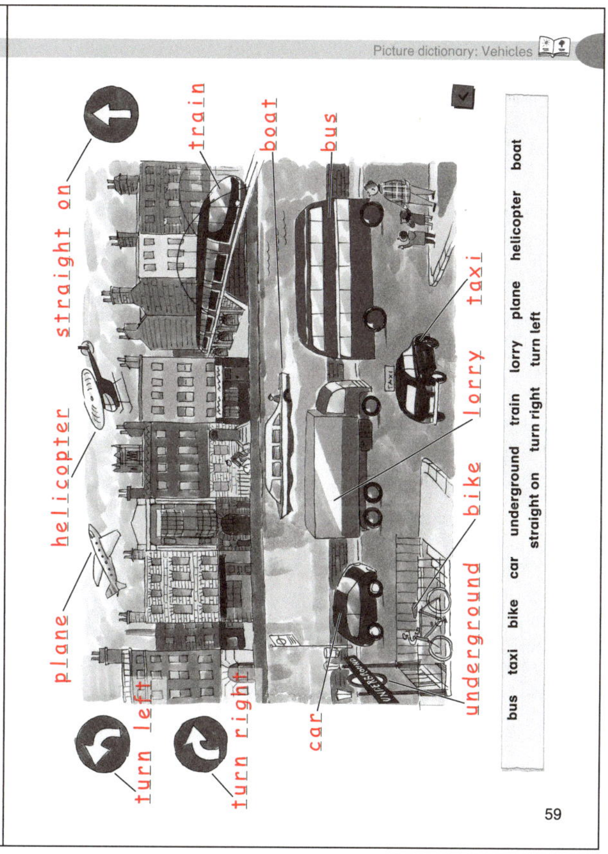
Picture dictionary: Vehicles
straight on
train
boat
bus
helicopter
plane
taxi
lorry
bike
underground
car
turn left
turn right
bus taxi bike car underground train lorry plane helicopter boat
straight on turn right turn left
59

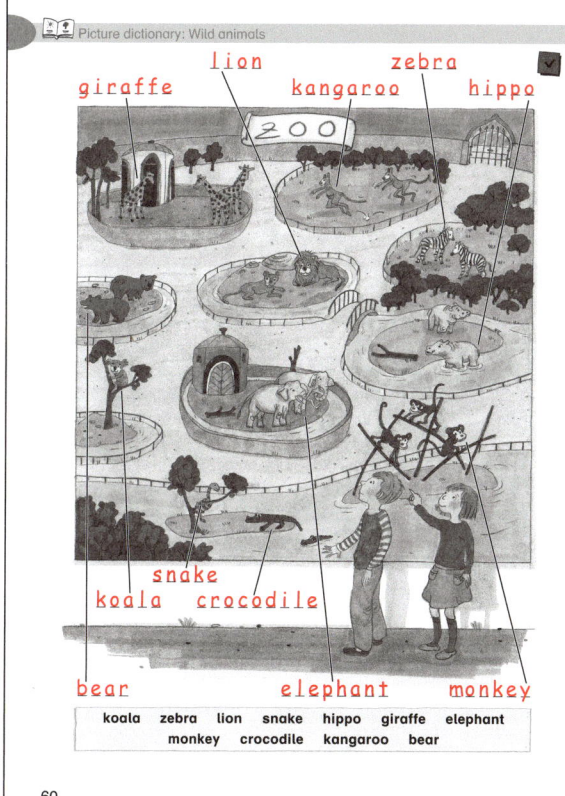

Picture dictionary: Wild animals
giraffe
lion
kangaroo
zebra
hippo
ZOO
snake
koala
crocodile
bear
elephant
monkey
koala zebra lion snake hippo giraffe elephant
monkey crocodile kangaroo bear
60

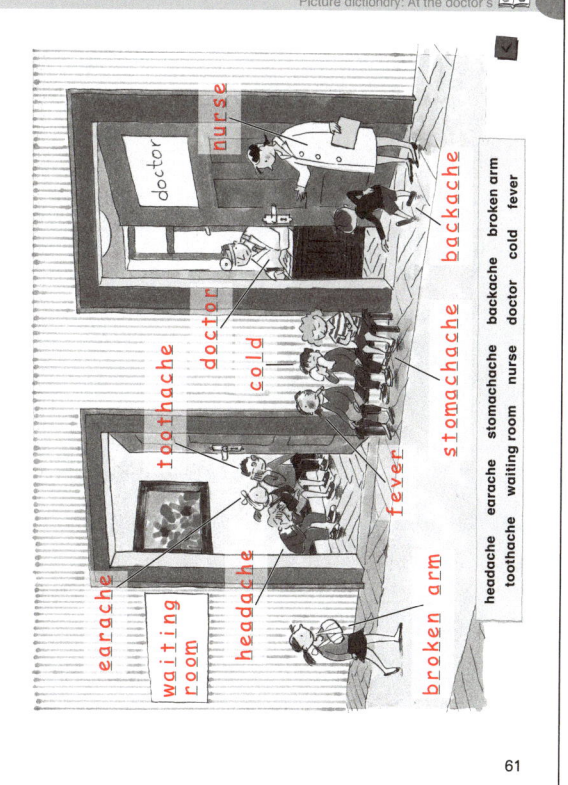

Picture dictionary: At the doctor's
nurse
doctor
backache
doctor
cold
toothache
stomachache
fever
earache
waiting room
headache
broken arm
headache earache stomachache backache broken arm
toothache waiting room nurse doctor cold fever
61

Lösungen

Jobs ✓

| shop assistant | hairdresser | teacher | doctor |
| policewoman/policeman | actress/actor | vet | football player |

teacher   hairdresser   actress

football player   doctor   actor

vet

policeman
policewoman   shop assistant

Jobs at home ✓

I...

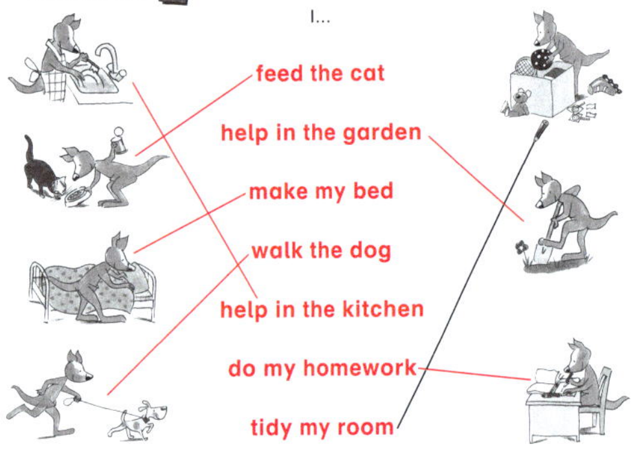

- feed the cat
- help in the garden
- make my bed
- walk the dog
- help in the kitchen
- do my homework
- tidy my room

62

Germany   France   Great Britain

Spain   Poland   Turkey

Italy   USA   Russia

| Italy | Great Britain | Turkey | USA (United States of America) |
| Germany | Russia | Poland | Spain | France |

63

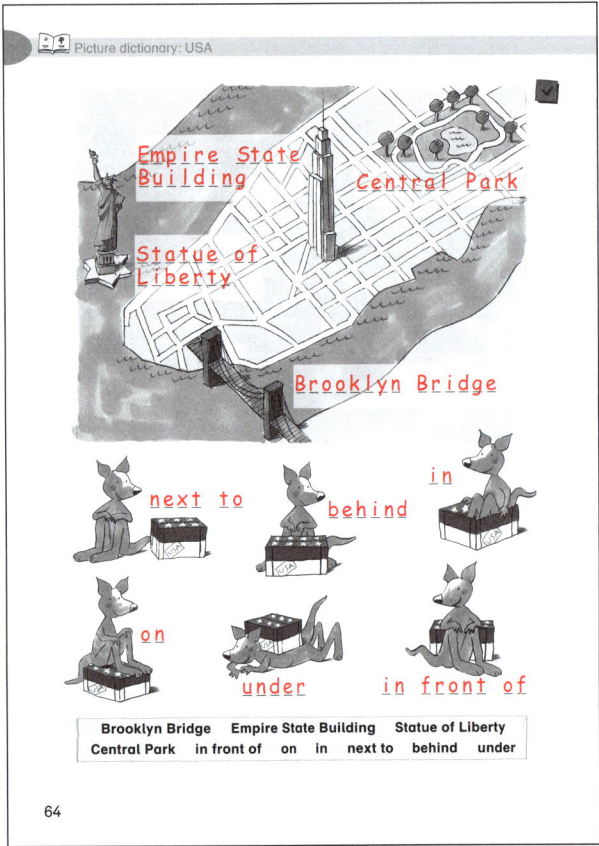

Empire State Building   Central Park

Statue of Liberty

Brooklyn Bridge

next to   behind   in

on   under   in front of

| Brooklyn Bridge | Empire State Building | Statue of Liberty |
| Central Park | in front of | on | in | next to | behind | under |

64

_ _ _ _ _ _ _   _ _ _ _ _ _ _   _ _ _ _ _ _ _

_ _ _ _ _ _   _ _ _ _ _ _ _   _ _ _ _ _ _

_ _ _ _ _   _ _ _ _   _ _ _ _ _ _

| Italy | Great Britain | Turkey | USA (United States of America) |
| Germany | Russia | Poland | Spain | France |

| Brooklyn Bridge | Empire State Building | Statue of Liberty |
| Central Park | in front of | on | in | next to | behind | under |